T0129966

All You Need To Do Is Change Your Thoughts To Live Your Dreams

The Power In You Is Greater Than Great. The Greatest Gift From God

Sandra Pearsall

author HOUSE®

AuthorHouse™
1663 Liberty Drive
Bloomington, IN 47403
www.authorhouse.com
Phone: 1 (800) 839-8640

Published by AuthorHouse 11/15/2019

ISBN: 978-1-7283-3608-4 (sc)
ISBN: 978-1-7283-3607-7 (e)

Print information available on the last page.

Biography

Sandra Pearsall was born in Baltimore Maryland, January 9, 1971. Family very poor on welfare. Experienced very hard times living in abusive homes. She was an outstanding student top of her class. At age 16 Sandra was a virgin held against her will beat raped for days. Pregnancy resulted from the rape. Later she had a miscarriage. Too afraid to tell the man continue to stalk, beat and rape Sandra until she dropped out of high school and ran away to save her life.

Sandra got a job immediately at KFC. Received her high school diploma after taking the GED exam. She also became a Certified Nursing Assistant after paying for her class with her first paycheck from KFC. Sandra admits it was scary out there alone but God was with her. She landed a job at the Nursing home earning $5.25/hr almost $2 more than KFC.

Sandra was able to get a studio apartment for $250/ Month.

This book is about how you can use your God given powers already in you to have all that you really want in life. You can live your dreams and be happy. This great power in you is for good. To have health, wealth, happiness, love, money, and a whole lot more.

I show you in this book how to change those negative thought that's destroying your life. I teach you how to think to prosper and have all the money you desire.

God is your supplier and is ready to supply all of your needs.

Other Books By Sandra Pearsall

First Book "Let Real Estate Work For You As It's Doing For Me"

By Sandra Pearsall

Www.authorhouse.com

1888-280-7715

 AS SEEN ON TV

Sandra Pearsall

NO
MORE
REAL ESTATE
SECRETS

This is a straightforward guide to Real Estate investing. Learn how Sandra used $500 to acquire 14 properties, retire at age 34 and build her empire.

Second Book "No More Real Estate Secrets"

By Sandra Pearsall

www.authorhouse.com

1-888-280-7715

God and The Universe is always working even while you are sleeping.

This is a fact whether you believe it or not.

If I knew 20 years ago what I know today I would be a Billionaire today.

I am pleased to share this discovery and my personal experience in hopes you receive and follow the information that totally changed my life.

No one has to live without the luxuries of life. A wise man once said it's a sin to be poor.

It doesn't matter your education level, it doesn't matter your race, sex, gender, your background.

It really does work.

I am 48 years old today and this is the most happiest and peaceful I've been my whole life. I don't worry about anything. I know God is my supplier and will supply my every need and want in infinite abundance.

These are a few properties I purchased with only the help of God.

As of today Sandra has purchased 15 houses, reached financial freedom at age 34. She's a Landlord, Real Estate Investor, Self publishing Author, Motivator, Speaker, Clinical Pharmacy Technician, Artist and Educator. Sandra is full of information, happy to share, and still very humble to this day.

Sandra Pearsall has been seen on TV, Fox 45, UPN 24, WBAL TV, 92Q Radio, DC Radio Station with Sherman Ragland, Black Enterprise Magazine, Essence Magazine, Say So Magazine, The New York Times, The Baltimore Times, The Carroll County Times, Women Shaping The World event in New York, The Blooms-berry Review, Real Estate Magazine and much more

Sandra is known for having a kind given heart, very spiritual, positive, hard working and strong belief in God. She believes God gave man the best gift in the world. A powerful mind. Sandra says she has been using the power of her mind before she even learned about how powerful the mind is.

Awarded Baltimore's Top Real Estate Investor

I Sandra Pearsall want you to know from this day forward there's a great power in us all. You just need to know how it work and do as I say. I went from being homeless, feeling helpless, earning $3.35 per hour to one day purchasing 15 houses from Maryland to North Carolina. While working a full-time job in the pharmacy, running my own cleaning service, wrote and self published 2 books on the subject of real estate. Helped so many people to buy their first homes. Never owned a real estate license. You do not need a real estate license to be a real estate investor. That's usually one of the first questions people ask me. You do not need a real estate license to invest in real estate. In 2006 I was awarded Top Investor in the Nation by George Ross/ Donald Trump Mentor at the DCREIA in Bowie Maryland. My first book entitled "Let Real Estate Work For You As It's Doing For Me" reached the top sellers list.

I reached financial freedom by the time I was 34 years old. Then I wrote my second book entitled "No More Real Estate Secrets"

I was able to inspire and encourage people to be great. I shared with people anything that I could to make sure they was a success also.

There are people who know things but will not share the information. Many of them are very well off even some millionaires and billionaires.

You have to get up and make it happen for yourself. I use to hope that someone would discover me to help my books go viral. I wrote letters to all the big time talk show host, e mails, mailed my information. I even spent $17,000 for a half page ad for one month in a major magazine.

At that time I had a lot of success from real estate investing and social media and local media was not getting me the exposure I needed.

Little that I knew I was looking to be discovered but I had already been discovered and created by The Almighty God.

I spent many years trying to market myself to the most famous people until I realized God is more famous than anyone in this world.

No one is coming to save you but Jesus.

I know that for sure.

Always go to God first. We tend to call on God after we have went through our whole cell phone list of contacts to talk to. No one can help you like God can. No one love you the way God does.

Make God first before you and anyone else.

Be a giver. Give more than you take. All that you give come back to you multiplied. When you give make sure you are giving from your heart. I don't look for praise of recognition for what I give. God see everything that you do. You will be rewarded.

I do want to speak on a very important topic. Make sure if you work a job you are doing a labor of love. If you go to work everyday to a job you hate and is only there to earn money that causes stress, anxiety, depression, sadness, and causes problems at home.

Prayer and Meditation will unlock your best gifts and you'll find who you really are.

Try to find peace at everything that you do.

Workplace stress kills thousands every year. I've been a healthcare worker now since 1988 and have seen a lot.

I have seen people pushed over the edge to mental breakdowns, to strokes from high blood pressure, to heart attacks and even deaths from workplace stress.

I have worked places in my lifetime where you work 8 hours no breaks, no lunch, the whole day has gone by and you realize you have not even had time to go to the bathroom.

If you are that person change that cycle even if you have to change jobs. You are not doing right by your mind, body, and soul. You'll always feel unhappy under those conditions.

Heart disease is still the number 1 killer in the United States. Take care of your heart. Always remember you are not a tree. You are not stuck anywhere. You can move anytime.

The affirmations I talk about later will help you with getting stronger, respecting and appreciating yourself, and knowing how worthy you are.

Be that person who is kind to all. God want us to be more like Jesus. People go their whole lives without this information. God know we are not perfect that we were born in sin. It was not your fault you were born in sin. Be the best person you can be and God will continue to bless you in so many ways.

Jesus was obedient to God. Your most important job on earth is to be obedient to God. When you pray remember to pray for others. Jesus was not selfish. What I'm sharing with you is so important in order for things to come to you.

Have a positive mental attitude.

When you wake up in the morning praise God. Before I get out of bed I speak Thank you God for this day. I will rejoice in this day.

You will automatically feel better no matter what your day will be like.

Expect to have a great day. If you expect to have a bad day it will be bad. So expect to have a great day.

Make sure you understand if you are under attack it's because you are good. You are doing some good and pleasing to God.

This is not your battle. Recognize it right away and give it to God. Do not try to fight that battle. Stop and pray.

The good will always be attack. I need for you to really understand this. You did nothing wrong to deserve the attacks. The devil don't play fair and will attack you at your weakest point. The devil will use your husband, wife, children, close friends, anything known to hurt you. Give it to God. I always say let go and let God. This goes way back to the first murder on earth. Two Brothers Cain and Abel. Cain was mean and selfish but his little brother was good, kind and caring. Cain offered God his worse he felt God don't need his best. Abel offered God his best. God was very pleased with Abel. Cain decided to kill his brother out of jealousy. I always tell people about this because it gives you a better understanding why you may be under attack at home, at work, in school, in church or anywhere. Give it to God. Let go and let God.

Fear is a factor that holds most people back in life. Fear if something is not going to work out. Fear if it's something that can really be done. Most of all it's easy to take on the fear of other people. Family and close friends. Whenever we have a great Idea we tend to go to get someone else opinion about something you want to do. After you hear their negative response it just add to your own fear. Do you know most of the time we are asking the opinion of someone who has no idea what you are talking about.

God is in you. Believe. I say a prayer everyday. I say Lord God and The universe thank you for my blessings I have already received and those blessings that are on the way. I am very grateful. I am ready to have and receive $1,000,000.00 now. I plan to do right by my money blessing. I know that's it's on the way. I have no doubt no fear nor worry.

God I know and accept that you are my supplier. You always supply my everyday need. I thank you. In Jesus name I pray. Amen! Thank you.

The best advice I can give you is whatever you have in mind you want to do it's important to do your own research. Online is a excellent tool. Get around people who are doing what you want to do.

This God given power that most people never know about in a lifetime. A Power for Good. A power so powerful you can shake the earth.

You were created by God in the image of God. That's a very powerful truth. You can go back to your Bible to check me. I want to share with you just by a matter of changing your thoughts everything in your life will automatically begin to change.

I know what it's like to be broke, hungry, sick, never having enough of anything. Having to work 2 or 3 jobs just to half way make it. Stand on the corner in the extreme cold waiting for the public bus freezing in the snow.

Trust me I know what it's like to be homeless and no where to turn. The women shelter too full so they have to turn you away. I will never forget the day the worker at the men's homeless was so kind to let me come in to sit down and eat a hot meal with the homeless men. I can still remember how good the soup and biscuits was. The first thing we did was hold hands and pray. It reminded me that God is alive.

I wanted to tell my story many years ago but I was so embarrassed even though I did nothing wrong. It's so important for me to share this because it can be life-changing for someone or so many.

I had really low self esteem. Growing up poor Black and experiencing so much abuse. Because of my dark skin I was considered black and ugly. In the 70's and 80's was horrible for me. I began to believe I was ugly because of my dark skin. I even remember when I was a kid trying to wash some of the black off of my face so I could be pretty. Everyone on TV who was pretty was white women. When Oprah showed up on the news station who looked like me I watched her everyday.

Even her talk show. Oprah has been one of the biggest life long inspirations.

I feel good about myself now. I had to learn to love myself. Michelle Obama has also been a big inspiration in my life. We have to teach the children to love themselves. You can't love God if you don't love yourself. God created you.

You are suppose to be happy, you are suppose to be healthy, wealthy, and doing a labor of love. You suppose to have everything you want and desire in infinite abundance. This is God promise to you at birth.

It's your personal mindset that keep you broke or in the position you are in today. The words you speak will keep you in poverty.

Allowing other people to feed your mind negativity will totally destroy you slowly.

You may have to remove those people who are very negative people in your life. They will stop your blessings from coming.

You have to have a calm mind and have no interruptions in your life with negativity.

Spend more time with yourself. It's truly worth it in the long run. The positive changes in you life will be noticeable to family, friends, co workers, and even strangers.

That powerful positive God spirit in you is going to shine.

When you take a work break of lunch take time for prayer and meditation. You can afford to skip several meals but you can afford to skip a few minutes of prayer and meditation.

Whether you believe me or not we can speak things into existence. I did not make this stuff up. I been doing it for years without even knowing it. Now that I have more knowledge things happen faster.

Why do you think God said Let the weak say I'm Strong. Your spoken words are super powerful. Your spoken words can change your life. If you speak negative most of the time you will have a lot of negative things come your way. If you learn to speak more positive and think more positive you'll see positive changes in your life.

Poor people stay poor because the mind of a poor person is normally in a poor mode.

There are just a few things you have to do that will change your life. Trust me it has changed my life. The very best thing I can do for you is share this powerful information with you. I hope you share this book with others. The more people you bless the more blessings you'll receive. God is a good God. In The Name of Jesus. Amen.

I have been studying the Bible my whole life, I have read motivational book after book. Attended Seminar after seminar trying to figure out why so many people never receive while some tend to have everything in infinite abundance. I turned my car into a mobile classroom. I have a PhD in self education. What I am going to teach you in my book no school will teach you this. You can go to the best University graduate with a 4.0 GPA and thats all great. So many people struggle finding jobs after investing so much time in school. It just didn't make sense to me I had to find out what is it. Why is it this way. My many many years of self education lead me to my spiritual self. The very powerful, blessed, beautiful, unstoppable, incredible, amazing self.

Everyday take time out of your schedule for prayer and meditation. This is so powerful for your mind, body and soul. You will look better, feel better, sleep better, everything will be better. Prayer and meditation connects you to God, The Universe, and Your powerful being. Do it twice a day. Morning and at night for at least 30 minutes.

Read this book from cover to cover. Read it more than just once or twice. These life changing things I share is so simple if you just do as I say you will begin to receive all the Blessings from God you ask for. Live a richer life full of prosperity. People tell me all the time everything I touch turns to Gold. The law of attraction is real. God universal laws are real. They exist even if you don't understand them all.

My mentor once said formal education will earn you a living but self education will earn you a fortune. I received.

Ask Believe Receive.

I promise I will make this information as simple as possible. Even a child can follow. You will not have to read 300 or 400 pages and still have no clue what to do. Some authors love to write and publish very large books and thats fine. If you anything like me I want some answers as quickly as possible or I will lose interest in the first several chapters.

When you are paying your bills have a happy attitude. Don't complain about having to pay the bill.

Speak out loud or in your mind that all the money I use to pay my bills will circulate back to me in infinite abundance. I was very skeptical in the beginning but things started happening. I started getting checks in the mail from multiple sources just like I had studied about. The sooner you begin the sooner you'll begin to have results. Have a positive attitude about yourself. Create a better relationship with money.

Everyday life can be very stressful but you can change that by changing your habits. When you wake up in the morning and plan to have a great day but the first thing you do is turn on the morning news. After hearing about so many people getting shot, a newborn baby found in the dumpster, a fatal car crash near by, someone home burned down. Now you can't understand why it's only 8:00am in the morning and you feel totally stressed out. Stop feeding your mind negativity. When you stop doing those things that keep you poor and stressed out you'll begin to live a more prosperous life.

The morning news is not the way to begin your day. Leave the TV off. This is the best time to get in a morning prayer and meditation. Think about all the things you would like to have in your life. Close your eyes and vision that you already have it. That you already have the dream home, the dream car, the dream cashflow, the great health, the wonderful family. You can have it all. Now you have just put some very positive things in your thought for the day instead of something negative. I can not speak enough about how important your thoughts are. Gossiping will hold back your prosperity. If a co worker or friend want to bring gossip to you. Just say I'm sorry I am very busy. You want to keep a positive frequency going.

If you can believe you can have it. If you can vision it you can have it. Change your thoughts to change your life.

It doesn't matter where you are in life remember you can have what you really desire. When you tune into your spiritual self, God, and the universe miracles began to happen.

Put all of your trust in God. People tend to feel that their jobs are their suppliers. God is your supplier, your source, and God will supply all of your every needs.

Speak it before you go to sleep at night and as soon as you wake up. Say God is my supplier and God will supply all of my needs. I have no fear nor worry. Everything I want and desire God will send it to me in infinite abundance. Thank you.

All you have to do is Ask, Believe, Receive.

We all know how to ask the reason we don't always receive is that the belief system is so low. Everyday increase your faith. What helped me the most is self talk. I self talk everyday. It's a proven technique that help your belief systems and a great way to feel more powerful. Compliment yourself, love yourself, be good to yourself, appreciate the way God created you.

When you complain about yourself you are really complaining about the way God created you. You need to always be grateful for what you already have and God will bless you with more. No one is perfect but we can self improve everyday.

Self Talk/Affirmations

You can self talk in your mind, out loud, even write it down. It's very powerful for getting the things you want. Start your morning out with your affirmations. Say them several times a day. You will begin to memorized them and it will become automatic. You'll find yourself speaking your affirmations while driving to work instead of listening to the radio. You will feel less stressful because you will start feeling good even feel when something good is about to happen. It may be a promotion on the job you been wanting, a unexpected raise, a pre approval from the bank to buy a home. It could be almost anything good and you'll began to feel it in your soul. Whenever you receive something say thank you and mean it.

I'm not going to go too deep into it. I don't want to confuse you but what is happening you are tuning into a natural power source in the universe that works every time. When God created earth God created laws. Take the law of gravity. We really don't know how all this stuff work but it works. The law of gravity will work no matter if you are a good person or a bad person.

If the good person and the bad person both jumped out a 20 story building they both will hit the ground hard most likely be dead. So it doesn't matter the law of gravity work.

Say:

I am a Child of God

I feel fantastic

I am well

I believe in the God in me

God loves me

I am powerful

I am intelligent

I am amazing

I am grateful

I am beautiful

I am healthy

I am wealthy

I am very blessed

I expect all good to come to me now

I am very skillful

I am love

I have a Millionaire Mind

I am a Millionaire

Money is always circulating back to me

I have many talents

I am rich

I am unstoppable

I am happy

Money is good

Money help a-lot of people

Money is coming to me

Everyday I get richer

I am caring

I expect a money blessing any day now

I have a great relationship at home

I get better everyday

I am on my way to greatness

My life is changing for the good

I am fearless

I can do and have anything that I want

Nothing will stop me from prosperity

I am always thankful

I have plenty money

These affirmations play a major role. You are placing things great things into your subconscious mind. Your subconscious mind is working while you are sleeping.

There are scientific proof that people are healing themselves by thinking I am well, I am healthy, I feel better everyday.

When you have these affirmations in your subconscious mind things began to happen. Miracles began to happen. Life start to look better everyday. You will start appreciating things you never thought about before. You'll feel good inside and it will reflect on the outside.

I am living proof this is true. This is why I wanted to put this book together for you. People say what you don't know don't hurt. Trust and believe what you don't know does hurt. It hurt your health, your life, your family, your bank account and more.

You need to know the truth. God want you to have all that you want and desire. Money is not bad and is not the source to all evil. Money is good. Never worship money. Have a good relationship with money and it will circulate right to you.

If you keep believing that money is bad and the source to all evil you'll never have it. Money will not come to you.

God want you to have money. God don't want you to not have. God want you to have all the wealth you desire.

In the beginning It sounded weird that I was saying these affirmations. Especially the affirmations about money. I was still studying God, and the Universal laws at the same time I started incorporating these techniques in my life. I realized that the most important life changing thing most people will never know.

I was speaking these great things about myself. After about 2 weeks it no longer sound weird. The more I said my affirmations the more I began to believe what I was saying. The more real it became.

What next was unbelievable. I began to go to my mail box and inside I had unexpected checks from places on a regular. Some of the checks was small and some of the checks was large. I am very serious. I received checks from so many class action lawsuits on products I had purchased more than 2 years prior. The insurance companies with checks for over payments. Payroll correction checks. I can go on and on. I remember looking down and I was standing on a $20 bill. I went to walmart with my aunt one evening. I really did not feel like going but I did not want her to go alone. As I open the door there was $300.00 just folded up on the parking lot. I originally thought it was a trick with those fake bills people have. I picked it up and yes it was $300.00.

Anytime I ever received anything no matter what it is I always say thank you.

Thank you mean you accept the gift and is very grateful for it. More will come. Always remember to say thank you.

Something I have always said that is so true if you can dream it you can make it happen. Never give up on your dream. Place more thought into your dreams during the day than anything else. Think about what you really want several times a day. Do not get pulled into anything negative at work or at home. You don't want nothing to mess up your positive frequency.

Today is the day you must commit to changing your attitude in order to get the most out of your life. To have all that you want in infinite abundance. If the person you are with is not on board it's ok. Clear your mind of all those negative thoughts. Replace them with positive thoughts. It's normal to have a negative thought but you can change that thought just like that.

A journey of 1000 miles begin with a single step.

People have a-lot of failure in life due to lack of the right knowledge.

Before I knew this God like power in me I use to ask myself why is life so hard. I am so so tired. I had tried almost every Network Marketing business out there. I know for sure I tried at least 60 of them and worked it really hard but never had the results I wanted. I would maybe make back my initial invested to get started sometimes not.

The jobs tend to want you to do more and more everyday. Many expect you to do impossible task in 8 hours. It's impossible to do 12 hours of work in 8 hours. Many jobs are only concerned about the budget and profit. They normally will never pay you what you are worth. Less likely appreciate you for what you do everyday. You are expected to give a certain amount of time to resign but the job can let you go without warning.

This is why I share this amazing information about your inner self your spiritual self so you can have positive life changing experiences.

This information I'm sharing with you is not new. It's far from new.

Many jobs causes you to feel bad or have a negative spirit which result in years of negative experiences.

How many times your boss remind you of how many applications he/she has on their desk.

You are told not to come to work sick but if you take off sick you get a write up. Now your Job is on the line. I have nothing against having a job. You must make sure you are happy on your job and is not depending on the job for your livelihood.

You need to know you have the power to have all that you want and desire without putting your trust in a job. Your trust need to always be in God.

I have worked basically since I was 13 years old. The Summer jobs for low income families. I never had a childhood. I am thankful because I know it could have been even worse.

There's a bright side to every situation. I am not afraid to fail. I take risk all the time. I know if I don't risk going far I will never know how far I can go. The more I increased faith the more success I have.

For you to even get started with your new life of good health, wealth, love, peace, happiness and prosperity. You will need to truly forgive everyone who has hurt you in any way or form. Get it out of your system.
Don't hold no bad feelings for anyone. It can be hard but it's a must so that you can move forward to prosperity.

Climb out of the past to move forward.

You have to go deep down in your heart and soul. Forgive your parents for wrong doing, forgive anyone who has harmed you, forgive the person or persons on your job who has harassed you, forgive the ex husband, wife, boyfriend, girlfriend, children. Forgive them all by name. Also ask God to forgive you for your sins and forgive you if you hurt someone knowingly or unknowingly. That you are ready for the life that God promised you at birth. In Jesus name Amen!

Too many people are stuck living in the past. They talk about the past all the time. Feel sorry for themselves. You must get rid of all of that in order to get the most out of life.

Stop blaming others for your short comings. Get rid of that blame list. At this point in your life you have the power to live better. You are responsible for your own life. Everyday check your own attitude. See if we are so focused of the attitudes of others we neglect to see what we are doing wrong.

Those affirmations will help with changing you to have a better attitude.

Having a bad attitude along with living in the past causes lack of success, lack of true happiness, depression, anxiety, all kinds of health problems and it's passed down to the children and their children it's like a toxic cycle.

With the law of the universe you get more of what you throw out there. whatever you complain about you are going to get more of if. Whatever you constantly think about and speak about you'll get more of it.

I hear women all the time talk about they keep getting the same kind of man. If you are always speaking about what you don't want in a man you are speaking that don't want man in your life.

You need to change what you speak. Speak only what you want in that man. If you want a loving, caring, smart, strong, compassionate, career man. These are the words you speak. Most say things like I don't want no broke man looking to live off me.

Never speak like that again. You are not aware that you are speaking the wrong man in your life.

The same goes for men. I hear them talk about gold diggers. They don't want them but that's all they talk about.

Let that sink in.

This is why you must change your thoughts and your words. God gave us the power to speak things into existence.

True story I use to say every time I am around children I get sick. Let me tell you every time I was around children I really got sick. I mean really sick. I had no idea I was making this happen from the words I was speaking.

The last time I said that a kid was sitting next to my desk at work. I was keeping a eye on him while his mother went for X-rays. Children were not allowed to go in that area. The nurse ask me if he could sit next to me because she was so busy. I said sure. I gave him some graham crackers and orange juice. I didn't even speak it. I was talking to the little boy but I thought it in my mind that every time I'm around little kids I get sick. I thought it you hear me. I did not even speak it. I got so sick that night. When I came to work the next day I could hardly breathe. The hospital admitted me for 3 days. I had fever, chills, lungs was so tight the breathing treatments would not work. I was getting breathing treatments every 2 hours, IV's, pills, IV steroids it was a mess.

This is how powerful your mind and thoughts are. You are doing some of the same things that I was doing but is not truly aware.

I use to say every time I get a new car someone is always trying to hit me. Do you know every new car I got someone hit me. Even one was totaled and I was never at fault. Well I was at fault because I was speaking into existence. I don't speak like that no more. I don't think like that no more.

How many times you have gone to the drive through and said I know they going to mess up my order. You get your food and it's totally wrong. It's not their fault. It's your fault.

I really want you to get this. I want you to receive. If you receive your life will be magical.

As a kid my mother was always hiding from the landlord or getting evicted. for years as a kid I thought the landlord was a sniper coming to kill us. No joke. I would be hiding behind the sofa and would not move. I remember coming home from school and everything we owned be sitting on the streets. Sometimes the neighbors would take us in. My mom had 8 kids so it was not easy to find someone to always take us all in.

You will be amazed at how your childhood plays a huge role on your thought process. The very first home I built was lovely. It was not huge but very nice. It was a 3 bedroom 2.5 bath 2 car garage. The builders was KB Homes.

I was always thinking I don't ever want to lose this home. Every month I paid the mortgage I was happy but I still had that negative thought in the back of my mind. I built that house in 2006 and live there for years. The bottom fell out of real estate I lost my home to foreclosure in 2013. It was my mind, my thoughts, my mental attitude that cause me to lose my home.

I'm not going to take too much time with my examples but I just want you to realize so many things that you may be experiencing is your own fault. Knowing my story will encourage you to stop immediately what you are doing now and change.

The positive side of this all I learned from all of my mistakes and began to empower my mind and control my thoughts. If I had a negative thought I would change that thought immediately. My life has changed and I am living life to the fullest.

I went into deep prayer and meditation. I was depressed, stressed, sad, confused, just an emotional reck. I cried one day for about 6 hours straight. This was suppose to happen for me to be here to tell you it can change. You can change everything. You can be and have all God blessings.

This is what lead me to find the most powerful information that I am sharing with you today.

I decided to turn off my cell phone, get off social media, turned off the TV, and radio.

I went on a spiritual quest to find out what is really going on. Why am I here, what is my purpose of being here.

I wanted to know why so many good people work so hard all their lives and can barely get by. I said I'm a good person, hard working, child of God, always helping people, very caring but I just could not figure out what I was doing wrong.

I found this book Think and Grow Rich by Napoleon Hill. I read this book from cover to cover. Amazing discovery. Something caught my eye in the book. He made a statement Whatever Your Mind Can Conceive And Believe The Mind Can Achieve. That was a eye opener. I started comparing this book to the Bible and finding that we can paint our lives with our Mind. For the next 5 years I did research on Mind Power, Law of Attraction, God Universal laws. I began to do exactly what I was learning.

Nothing I had come across was different from my faith in God. This was placing me closer to God on a very spiritual side. I began to appreciate the rain. Things that would normally upset me no longer was upsetting. The world started looking different. Very peaceful. The affirmations I was speaking everyday was making me more positive.

I started believing in myself. Positive things started to happen to me. I was so super excited I was trying to tell everybody what I had discovered.

Everything was truly coming together very amazing. My friend gave me a book called The Secret by Rhonda Byrne a great book. It was like information started coming to me and I no longer had to search. I was searching for answers then God started sending answers to me everyday. I was introduced to Bob Proctor from the book The secret. I began doing his guided meditations twice a day. What a difference the power of meditation does for the mind, body, and soul. Then shortly after one morning a pop up of Earl Shoaff-How to be a Millionaire popped up on my screen. I clicked on it. Wow! Life Changing.

I first created a dream board. I had $17 in my bank account at this time but that didn't matter to me. My faith was very strong. My mind had become super powerful. My belief system in God was one hundred times stronger than before. With the knowledge I had obtained daily prayer, meditation and affirmations. It was on. I placed my dream board on the wall next to my bed. I believed.

I put I want a brand new home built from ground up in 2019, I describe the home I wanted. I was not concerned where I was going to get money from. I knew if I worry my dream was not going to come. I described everything I wanted in the new home. I could see it already finished. I could see in my mind the nice hard woods floors to match the kitchen cabinets. I'm telling you this because you need to be able to visualize it. I could see the master bath with double sink. Keep in mind I could see all of this with $17 in my savings account. I placed the board where I could see it before I closed my eyes for sleep at night. You need to put on your board everything you want and desire now. When you finish write Thank You. I added I wanted a brand new 2019 Toyota Camry, with black with Crome trim. I wanted Ash Grey interior. I Ask for a better relationship with my man, financial freedom, to lose 100 pounds. I have always dreamed of being a Millionaire. I wrote myself a check for $1,000,000.00 to look at every day and night.

This is exactly how you plant your seeds.

Visualize it, write it down, describe it in details, write Thank you. Thank you mean you accept your blessings.

You can do the same on paper. Write everything down, write and say thank you and put the paper away. It will begin the process.

In less than 1 year major events began to happen. Everything good started coming to me. Good Health. No longer had to take diabetes medicine. Perfect labs. I loss 60 pounds. I received a unexpected money blessing. I was able to build that dream 2019 home that I wanted. It's exactly what I saw in my vision. That 3 bedroom, 2.5 Bath, 2 Car Garage, Wood floors the same color of the kitchen cabinets. My relationship with my man improved 100%. We are very happy together. I was able to purchase that 2019 Toyota Camry that I ask for. Thank you God and The Universe.

2019 Newly Built Home. Thank you

2019 Brand New 2019 Toyota Camry Thank you

I Lost 60 pounds after weight loss surgery Thank You

The most amazing thing I found from meditation I had a hidden talent. The gift to create art. I never studied art nor taken any classes. One morning God spoke to me about 3:00am. Said create art. I have been creating art ever since and many of them are very good. I put on canvas or art paper from what I see in my mind. It has been very healing, relaxing and has also bought me peace.

Recently studies show that having art hanging around in the hospitals help the patients heal. One day I want to use my art to help people heal.

BEFORE   **AFTER**

This is a box of seeds that I have been planting. After I write down everything I ask for. I say Thank you. I write Thank You on the letter or note whatever you want to call it. I put it away to never open them again. True story and God and The Universe start working.

Thank you.

I am happy and grateful. I am happy to share this information to help others. I always wish for the best for myself, my family, my friends, and all those who

are in need. I am so happy and grateful that God lead me to finding out the secret of good health, love, happiness, wealth, and obtaining all that I want and desire. I am thankful for peace. Thank you

I expect my Million Dollar Check one day soon. Thank you

Make sure you think big.

You are born great. You have amazing powers locked up inside of you. Know that your mind is very powerful. Make sure to try to keep your mind as free as possible from negative energy.

Speak or read your affirmations everyday. It does not take long but is a very powerful tool. Positive energy is 100 times more powerful than negative energy.

Take care of your mind.

If you believe you can its true.

If you believe you can't thats also true too.

I really hope you use this information. My life has been transformed. I no longer major in minor things. I appreciate everything. It's a Blessing to be able to give to help someone. No matter how big or small.

I decided to love myself as myself as God created me. I no longer relax my hair. I wear my natural hair I was born with. At a young age I did not appreciate my hair. It was not straight enough. I was called nappy head or beady head. I never realized that I had a developed a complex about my own hair. There were no commercials on TV with Black hair other than getting a hair weave. The commercials always had beautiful white women with long straight hair with so much body I wondered why my hair did not look like that.

I'm telling you this because we all are beautiful. No matter long hair, short hair, straight, curly, or nappy. It is the parents responsibility to love their children and teach the children to love themselves. If you have freckles on your face that's your special signature from God. I am speaking of all races. Let's get rid of these stigmas from our children so they can grow up to love themselves and each other.

God sent me the love of my life. Marriage coming very soon 2020

A gift of art from God

Thank you

ART BY SANDRA PEARSALL

It's so amazing I'm in my 40's and discovered love, peace, labor of love, harmony, what truly make me happy, gifts to share with others. I wish this for all.

I have always loved helping people with whatever I can it's just in my nature from when I was a kid. I thank God for a caring spirit.

I have been working in the Hospital Pharmacy and Home Infusion Pharmacy for 32 years.

I recently ran across a study that the hospitals are hanging more art around all the areas of the hospital. It's believed that art helps the patients to heal by giving them something beautiful to look at while healing. Now isn't that remarkable.

I hope my art have those same healing powers to help all of my readers. I pray for all of you to have a better life and enjoy living. In The name of Jesus. Amen. Thank you for your support.

You will be very amazed about all the gifts you have locked up inside of you.

Printed in the United States
By Bookmasters